# HOW TO FORGIVE ANYONE

*Simple Guide To: Forgiving Yourself And Those "Past Pains"*

Non-Denominational And Non-Confrontational

By
ROBYN IONA

COPYRIGHT © 2024
ROBYN IONA

All rights are reserved. No part of this book may be reproduced, distributed, or transmitted in any form or by any means, including photocopying, recording, or other electronic or mechanical methods, without the prior written permission of the author, except in the case of brief quotations embodied in critical reviews and certain other noncommercial uses permitted by copyright law.

ISBN 979-8-89342-388-4

# *Dedication*

*I am grateful to all participants who inflicted pain and heartache throughout my life. It was through forgiveness I found my peace and created the best version of myself.*

*Thank you.*

## *Special Thanks:*

Amandine Le Roux Handcock,

You are my dearest friend. Thank you for guiding me through this journey. I honor you and your persistence in keeping me accountable. Together, we made my dream come true, and I am forever grateful. I Love You Forever.

Kristina Kay Knight,

Thank you for being my best friend. I love your ability to create laughter through any circumstance that surrounds you. You are the shining light that lifts and inspires me. I am grateful for your love, support, and friendship. I love you forever.

Michael Card,

You are my soulmate. You are a powerful presence in my life, my mentor, and my guru in all things spiritual and physical. Whenever life gets cray-cray, you remind me of who I am and where I came from. Most of all, I am a Goddess! Thank you for your love, support, and friendship. I love you forever.

# *About The Author*

Robyn Iona grew up in a verbally abusive environment. It is no surprise that she attracted verbally abusive relationships up until her 50s. It was her unsuccessful suicide attempt that triggered her to look beyond the pain she lived in. She had a choice: continue being abused and live with consistent pain or educate herself. Educating herself was a wise decision; she learned why she allowed this pain to consume her life. She learned how to change her thought patterns, mindsets, and belief systems. Most importantly, she learned how to love herself. Her eyes were opened to the realization that life is full of choices, and it was time for her to make some new ones. From Quantum Physics to Neuropsychology and Hypnotherapy to Energy Crystal Healing, she exposed herself to many variations of healing. She successfully changed her personality just by thinking and acting differently, so much so that she created a new version of herself and became the person she always wanted to be.

Intuition made her aware that if she wanted to have continued success in this transformation of self, she must forgive her past pains. As uncomfortable as that might have been, it didn't stop her. In her quest to find a forgiveness process, she only encountered religious-based and confrontational formats. No, that was not going to work for her; she was not about to go face-to-face with anyone who hurt her. Why would she have to? There are no rules to forgiving someone. So, instead of getting discouraged, she created her own modality: a non-confrontational and non-denominational process. A simple step-by-step guide for forgiving yourself and anyone else. She has a secret to this process, and trust me, it works flawlessly.

Much love and blessings to you.

Reverend,

Erik D. Jordan

# Contents

Dedication ........................................................................... iii

Special Thanks: .................................................................. iv

About The Author ............................................................. v

Introduction: For Those Who Have Decided: ................ viii

Chapter 1: Are You Ready To Forgive? ............................ 1

Chapter 2: My Story ........................................................... 9

Chapter 3: Mindsets ........................................................... 23

   These Are A Few Of My Favorites: .............................. 31

Chapter 4: Your Thoughts Create Your Reality ............. 34

   Give This A Try: ............................................................. 37

Chapter 5: Living In The Present Moment .................... 41

Chapter 6: The Act Of Forgiving Yourself ..................... 52

   Things I Am No Longer Apologizing For: ................. 63

Chapter 7: Taking Responsibility For Your Happiness ... 66

Chapter 8: The Act Of Forgiving Those "Past Pains" ..... 72

Chapter 9: Giving Yourself Permission To Let Go ........ 81

Acknowledgments ............................................................. 93

# *Introduction:*
# *For Those Who Have Decided:*

1. I am tired of being "mad at the world."
2. Continuing to play the blame game does not change or fix my problems.
3. That "NO ONE" should have control over any part of my life or my decisions.
4. Yes, it is time to take responsibility for my happiness.
5. No one can make me feel, say, or do anything unless I allow them to.
6. I am the only person with the power to change how I think.
7. I always have a choice; every day is a new day to make new choices.
8. I am free to write my own set of rules.

It's not about them. It's about forgiving yourself
for enduring the pain they inflicted.

Your secret power is: IT'S NONE OF THEIR BUSINESS!

Some individuals believe that to forgive someone, you must confront the offender. This is inaccurate information. You forgive someone because your body is getting sick, your mind says stop thinking about this, and your heart is tired of pumping out the heartache.

"Continuously replaying painful moments and dialogues allow our past traumas to dictate our present, robbing us of our power to move forward. It's as though we're handing the reins over to those moments and, by extension, granting control to those who were part of that pain. They occupy a central space in our thoughts, overshadowing the here and now."

Did someone tell you that you must forgive someone face-to-face? I kept reading about how "they" say you must do it this way for forgiveness to work. I call bullshit! Who are "they" anyway? We are all individuals who deal with heartache and pain differently. Doesn't that give us the right to choose what is best for our broken hearts? Of course, it does. I kept thinking, "Why would I want to see this person or persons again just to say, 'I forgive you'?"

Yes, the pain they inflicted on you is very real. Having that person reciprocate should not be expected. In order to heal from this pain, forgiving yourself can have amazing physical and mental results. Forgiving without confrontation is just as powerful as forgiving in person. Knowing you have a choice to confront or not to confront may be the initiative you need to forgive someone.

Once, I told my ex-husband that I forgave him, and he said, "What? Why? Really?" He knew what the reasons were, but he chose to play dumb, which is his business, not mine. Not acknowledging the pain he inflicted on me only substantiated my reasons to forgive myself and not tell anyone about it. He didn't care whether I did or did not forgive him. It was up to me to decide what was best for my sanity.

The only rules you need to follow are the ones that give you peace and make you happy!

I crafted this book to be an inclusive and gentle guide—respecting all beliefs and offering a peaceful path to forgiveness without the need for direct contact with the person you are forgiving or any specific religious context.

While I find comfort in the universe and the presence of angels, I firmly believe that everyone's life journey and beliefs are their own sacred choice. This book honors your autonomy and supports you in navigating your unique path to letting go and healing.

## Chapter 1:
## *Are You Ready To Forgive?*

Most people understand that our past stories have made us who we are today. If you are weary of living in your past, forgiving the people who have hurt you has amazing consequences. My process is an uncomplicated guide created through extensive research into forgiving.

I wrote this book for ANYONE who has experienced betrayal, molestation, abandonment, deceit, disloyalty, fraud, manipulation, lies, and unresolved resentment issues. This book is about you deciding NOT to live with the pain someone has inflicted on you.

NO RULES say YOU MUST interact, inform, include, enlighten, participate, collaborate, or connect with the person or persons who hurt you. I understand that confronting the past can be difficult. This book is for those of you who recognize the benefits of forgiving outweigh the consequences of holding on to the pain.

Since the tender age of 5, I've extended forgiveness to 57 individuals, including family members and personal and professional relationships. This has brought me profound change, and I share this process in hopes that it may do the same for you.

This book is interactive. I intentionally placed blank lines throughout the book for you to add your own personal notes. If the name of a person you want to forgive pops into your head, feel free to use that space to write it down.

It is critical to pause and reflect: Do memories of those who've harmed you often enter your thoughts? When discussing your past, what emotions surfaced? Does it bring a wave of discomfort, or do you feel a sense of community in sharing these experiences with others who understand?

If recounting these stories no longer brings you peace or a sense of camaraderie, it might be an indication that you are ready to step onto the path of forgiveness. Many find themselves in a cycle of recounting their victimhood; this is a normal part of the healing process.

If speaking about your experiences makes you feel uneasy—be it feelings of shame, foolishness, disbelief from others, or a fit of lingering anger—it's important to acknowledge these feelings. They are the part of you that you have been navigating, perhaps for many years.

I will be offering questions throughout the chapters for you to ponder and answer any way you decide to. So, grab a pen.

Some people talk relentlessly about being the victim, and that is okay. This is part of the healing process and a common way to deal with pain. Are you uncomfortable talking about the things you have been through? Why? Are you embarrassed? Do you feel stupid? Do you feel that if you told someone you were angry, they wouldn't believe you? Are you still angry? How many years have you been reliving your past pains?

These were reflections I faced myself. I have navigated a maze of emotions across various situations. I was the quiet one about revealing what I was going through. I felt both embarrassed for enduring the conflict and stupid for allowing it to continue. I once confided in my ex-husband about personal stories I had experienced, only to have that information used against me. My journals were read and used against me as well. I would write what I really felt in a journal and then rip the pages out so I would not be judged on its context. Now, I have 50-plus journals to use as references when writing my memoirs.

I vividly recall being threatened at the innocent age of eight, being told that speaking up would land us both in jail—an intimidation tactic to maintain silence. When I eventually found the courage to speak out, my confession was met with disbelief and harsh words from my own grandmother, making the experience all the more harrowing.

The pain, valid as it was then, has aged 35-plus years. Eventually, the time came for me to release that narrative, to forgive—not because the actions were acceptable, but because holding onto them was preventing my own healing process. So, I forgave both my grandparents.

Being honest about how you are feeling regarding your past pain is important to the success of forgiving your person. If the pain happened last week, then you may need more time to process it, and it could be too soon to forgive.

Making the decision to forgive is huge! Should you, too, feel that you have dwelt long enough in the shadows of your past and are seeking a way forward, free from those binds, know that choosing to forgive is a momentous step.

Forgiving is not just an act of mercy toward others but a profound act of self-love and a commitment to one's mental and physical well-being. It is not about forgetting; it is about freeing oneself to live a full and present life.

Why do you want to forgive your past?
Be specific and detailed, feel the reasons, and acknowledge them.

My advice is:

> Do not tell anybody who you are forgiving!
> Especially that person!

First, it's NONE of anyone's business what you're doing! Secondly, family and friends may have the best intentions. They will instinctively tell you what and how THEY feel and give you THEIR opinions about what you should do! You know they will. They can't help themselves. This unsolicited advice may be an unconscious response; perhaps they have unresolved pains that need healing. Be the inspiration for others to witness—forgiveness can be life-changing.

Please understand that forgiving someone does not mean you will forget who and what hurt you. You may never forget, but you will have control over how it affects your everyday life. That is what forgiving did for me. I remember what happened, but it doesn't hurt anymore; it's just part of my past.

Please be aware of the voice in your head and notice if you are judging or criticizing yourself. It may be talking to you, trying to explain or justify why you allowed someone to hurt you. It is too easy to blame ourselves for why things happen to us. It is time for you to stop blaming yourself and learn how to move past this pain crap.

My favorite part of this process is NO confrontation with that person. Whew! I have never had good luck with confrontation. I talked weirdly, stuttered, and sounded dumber than the person who was hurting me. What I wished I would have said at that moment seemed to come to me after the conversation was over. I hated that!

I don't like confrontation because of my mother. You never talked back to her, gave your opinion, or said anything at all if it conflicted with her. If you did, then you would pay for it by getting a whipping. I would curl up like a ball to avoid being bruised from being hit too hard.

I have an instinct to protect those I love and have no problem confronting that situation, but when it comes to defending myself, I still have issues with doing that.

All you need to do during my forgiving process is use your imagination. You picture them in your mind, whatever, however you wish. You have infinite possibilities using your imagination. You have the power to control how they look. You can visualize them with no mouth, no face at all, or looking like a piece of cake! All you need is your imagination to make this work.

Okay, just saying "I forgive you" to someone was not enough for me either. I needed something more—something that would make me feel real and believable. I found a few ideas about forgiving, but nothing made me say, "Yes, this is the one for me!"

The Oxford Dictionary defines forgiveness as "an active process in which you make a conscious decision to let go of any negative feelings of someone whether they deserve it or not." Okay, how do you do that? What is the "active process"? Do you have to stand face-to-face? What if they are mean and scare you? What if they denied this ever happened? What if you didn't know them? What if they were no longer living?

I gathered enough ideas and information from my research. I was able to create a simple, easy-to-do script. After trying it out on a few fender benders I had in my bag of hurts, I forgave the biggies, like my grandparents and mother. I felt so good after forgiving them that I started checking people off my list. Because it worked so well for me, I decided to share it with the rest of the world.

If you could write your own rules, what would they be?
About your life? Your career? Your relationships?

_____
_____
_____
_____
_____
_____
_____
_____
_____
_____
_____
_____
_____
_____
_____
_____

## Chapter 2:
## My Story

When I look back at the many dramas that I had to overcome, I now know these gave me the knowledge to grow as a person, gain wisdom about myself, and share this wisdom with those who need it. Do not get me wrong; I think that I learned those lessons and got over the pain right away. It took me many, many years to get where I am now. I lived in the middle of pain with no hope of ever getting out. I kept drawing in the same situations and scenarios that gave me that pain.

Everyone has a story; I understand this. Some of you have had traumatic events that have scarred you, basically for life. Some of you have had situations in your life that were inappropriate and left you feeling vulnerable, feelings that made you think that you would never be able to trust anyone ever again. Note: There is no book or informational platform that will help you unless you really want to let go of the heartache. I can't promise you this book will cure any deep-rooted pain or trauma. I can promise you that my pains were real, and

I am sharing with you what I found and how I let go and forgave these "past pains."

_____
_____
_____
_____
_____
_____
_____
_____
_____
_____
_____
_____
_____
_____
_____
_____

My mother ran away from her misguided family at the early age of 17. She married, had a baby boy, and got divorced. As she was looking for love in all the wrong places, she gave birth to another baby boy, a baby girl, and another baby boy, all by different men and out of wedlock. She married again and had a girl and boy, and that was preceded by a divorce. She continued this trend and had two more girls out of wedlock with again two different men. Four boys and four girls, all before the age of thirty. Whew!

Having a hysterectomy, no more children were to be born. She was exceptionally beautiful, with long auburn hair and green eyes. This is probably why she was able to find four more different men who wanted to marry her, along with all eight of us kids. That always impressed me! Continuing with two more marriages, her last divorce was at the young age of seventy. Yes, normal, right?

Well, all I can say is that it created me, a loyal, trustworthy, gullible, naïve girl. Having daddy issues, low self-esteem, and believing what people said to be true. Why would they lie? I was a people pleaser who would do just about anything for you if you would like me! The best part is easy to manipulate and control. Come one, come all, this girl is wearing a sign!

I love my mother, and I have forgiven her several times for her misguided and warped upbringing of crazy religious beliefs and unstable mindsets. She did the best she could, considering her childhood. You believe what you are taught to believe, no matter how ridiculous it may be.

My life had always seemed sad; I found myself always reaching for a better way to think, a way to change my life so it would be a positive and happy life. And I had some great moments and memories; you could count them on one hand. It was always hard just to survive, hard to find trustworthy friends, hard to find family members who didn't judge you. How do you stay positive when all you have ever known and seen is pain? How do you go from being at the bottom of a deep, dark hole of continual sadness and rising towards the light? I didn't know the answer!

At my lowest point, there was a combination of experiences that happened within weeks of each other. I was going through a horrific divorce. This left my best friend (my dog, Lucy Lulu) and me homeless and without transportation. I was able to bring her to my part-time job, but that was uncomfortable for those around me.

It seemed the people in my life were not the friends to me that I was to them. There was so much betrayal, disloyalty, and disbelieving things said about me that were ridiculous to even fathom. This was all piling up all at once; it was overwhelming. I was confused, shattered, and felt lost and alone.

I had reached that level when nothing else mattered. I was so tired of crying, tired of thinking about the why. So tired of being surrounded by unsupportive, selfish sons of bitches and living in a world that brought me so much pain. So, I planned for Lucy to stay with my ex-husband; he was absolutely the worst when it came to loving people, but he loved and respected his dogs, so I knew she would be taken care of.

I tried to kill myself with sleeping pills. I felt so much despair and grief; I did not know what else to do. I figured whatever the repercussions would be, I would ask whoever was in charge, if anyone was in charge, to forgive me.

Two days later, I woke up. Ah, man! Well, that obviously did not work. I thought, "Shit!" What the hell was I going to do now? I hated the idea of being stuck with this heartache and those memories for the rest of my life. I did what every person does after they try to kill themselves: I went and picked up my dog and proceeded to sink even lower and deeper into a depression! Yay!

After several months of struggling to go to work, having no energy, no passion, and no friends, one day, I woke up and was pissed at myself! I realized that thinking the same way, day after day, will only give me the same results. True? I don't know what I was waiting for, someone who would drive up in a white limo and sweep me off my feet. Or maybe Thor would take me in his arms and, with his big powerful hammer, fly me up to his planet, far, far away from all this hell? Now that's a dream come true!

What brought me out of the deep black hole was forcing myself to get up and volunteer. I figured the only way to get out of my head was to help someone who was maybe worse off than I was. I found all kinds of opportunities to help others. And it worked. I realized there were a lot of people who were just as unhappy as I was.

I had two choices: one, accept and stay in this sad situation, or two, figure out "the why" by educating myself. I decided to educate myself. I wanted a life of less drama, a life to be proud of, a reason to get up in the morning, not because I needed to but because I wanted to. I started reading self-help books, anything that would teach me why I had low self-esteem and no confidence, why I was a needy people pleaser, and why I created this sad life.

I started to read and read and read some more. I became obsessed. I loved learning about how the human mind works, the way we think, and the way we act and react to different situations. I kept on reading, and before I knew it, I had read forty-one books in only 10 weeks.

This was so exciting to me; so many of my issues were starting to make sense. These books explained why I acted the way I did and why I attracted the same situations and people into my life over and over again. It was such a relief to know that most of my problems were not my fault. I am not blaming any one person; it has been a shared contribution to my upbringing and chosen participants. Yes, it does start with your childhood.

Even my money issues, as well as allowing relationships to take control of me and my life. I hated that I allowed all those things to happen, but I'm thankful at the same time. These were the big questions I had asked, and now I understand. I can say now with confidence that I am no longer that person. She will always be honored but never missed.

You have the power to change who you have become.

Who do you want to be?

Who do you want to be? This is an especially important question to ask yourself. If you could be anyone or create your own version of yourself, what does that look like? Can you see yourself in a world that is not surrounded by your "past pains"? Try this: write down anything you want, describe in detail what a wonderful life you wish you had. Do not be shy; no one else will read this, your eyes only, so be creative:

_____

_____

_____

_____

_____

_____

_____

_____

> You are an energy magnet; you bring to you
> whatever you are feeling on the inside.

This is assuming that you did some daydreaming: I hope you were able to look past (pun intended) the pains and see what your life could look like, to live in a world where you do not need to relive those memories ever again. It can be beautiful.

You may not believe this, but this is my world now. I honestly do not relive any of my trauma dramas. I love that I do not even think about the shit I went through. After forgiving them, it's kind of weird, but I don't care to; I don't want to; I don't have to; I choose not to give them a second thought.

This is the attitude I suggest you have while doing this forgiveness process. Do you know how it feels when you're right about something? That feeling of confidence, self-empowerment, like you could and would kick ass for someone or something you believed in, and you were right about? It is a great feeling, right?

Think of a time when you were right about something, a moment when you had the confidence to stand up for someone or something. A positive outcome came because you were not afraid to speak the truth. Remember the way you held your head up high; your chest puffed out just a little.

Close your eyes right now, well, after I finish this sentence, please. Feel that feeling; remember that moment when you were unstoppable. Okay, go ahead and try it; I will wait. I'm not going anywhere.

Do you feel it, the confidence, the self-empowerment? If only for a moment! Feel it.

Now, hold on to that feeling and, with your index finger and thumb, gently tug at your earlobe. Squeezing it gently, feel that confident feeling; puff out your chest if it helps you really feel the feeling. Do this for a few more minutes. Picture in your mind what it was that made you feel so proud. Because you are proud of yourself, whatever it was, remember the feeling while holding your earlobe. This is called anchoring; whenever you get tied up in a knot, hold your earlobe, close your eyes, and remember this feeling. Now, if you wish, write down in detail how wonderful it felt, the confident superhero that is you.

_____

_____

_____

_____

_____

_____

_____

_____

_____

_____

# Chapter 3: Mindsets

I hope you were able to remember a time when you kicked ass, had great confidence in yourself, and remembered how it felt. Were you able to capture that feeling? It is important to go back to that feeling time and time again when you are not feeling that way.

One way you can change the way you think is through your subconscious mind. This is the method I used to change what I believed to be true then into what I believe to be true now. "The belief in your mind is from the thought in your mind. All your experiences, events, conditions, and acts are the reactions of your subconscious mind to your thoughts," said Mr. Murphy.

For example, you're the CEO of a big company. You introduce a new product and service to your management team. Their job is to make this happen. The boss says to do it, and your team does it. Your conscious mind is the CEO; it gives the order, and your subconscious mind takes the order based on what your conscious mind accepts and believes as true.

Whatever you keep repeating in your mind, "I can't get over this," or "I can't change how I feel," then that is what your subconscious mind will make happen. You will never get over it, and you will never change how you feel; that is one of the jobs of your subconscious mind.

There is a study at Harvard that states that between the ages of 0 and 7, we acquire our current mindsets and beliefs. Whatever environment we grew up in, whoever raised us, we inherently would mirror their views. Their way of thinking has been carried down by earlier generations—our mothers, fathers, stepparents, aunts, uncles, siblings, cousins, grandparents, friends, teachers, and classmates. They all have influenced us in some way or another.

The reason I am telling you this is because the things we learned when we were young are still implanted in our subconscious mind. If you were told you were an idiot, then you grow up feeling like an idiot. I was told I would never have any common sense, which it turns out I have a ton of it! Ha Ha!

I was also called a dumb blonde growing up. The dumb blonde part was difficult because whenever I didn't know how to do something, I felt stupid asking for help, and I would end up looking like a dumb blonde anyway. Never be afraid to ask for help; asking only makes you look more intelligent because you learn how to do something right the first time.

The primary cause of unhappiness is not so much the situations themselves but the emotional thoughts and feelings we have towards them. We naturally attach ourselves to emotional situations.

When we think about our past pains, we keep playing our greatest hits, "oldies but goodies," and "the best of" mind recordings, which then keep those memories alive. This creates a mindset.

A mindset is like a record player; the needle represents the people who influenced you growing up. The grooves in the vinyl record create the creases that hold your belief systems. The depths of those indentations will be based on how repetitious your family's lyrics were and what you had to endure.

Take a few moments; can you think of a couple of mindsets that you want to change? Write them down and try to figure out who taught you to think that way. The more clarity you have on your chosen mindsets, the easier it will be to change them. For example:

A poverty mindset: Growing up without enough food and being told to eat everything on your plate because children are starving in China. If you didn't finish eating your dinner, then you were to finish it in the morning for breakfast and lunch until it was gone. I say, some things just need to be flushed down the toilet.

A wealth mindset: This would mean that people who are rich are bad people. They steal from the poor to make themselves richer. Money is evil. Money can't make you happy. You can't play sports because we have no money to pay a babysitter.

Negative mindset: If you grow up with a parent who was constantly complaining (I'm not naming names), I'm sure you know who it is by now. She thought everyone was out to get her; it was always someone else's fault. I am right, and they are wrong. You get the idea. What kind of mindsets do you still have from your childhood?

How you feel about anything is how you feel about everything.

How do you identify your mindsets and belief systems? Just by being aware of them, you begin to change them. It is really that easy. When you think of a thought or any thought, pay attention to how you are feeling while thinking about that thought. That feeling is what to be aware of. The feeling of that thought is your secret to changing it.

When you believe that you have the power to change your embedded mindset recordings and the choice to change the lyrics, you have become the writer, producer, director, and STAR of your own production. You are now able to create a whole new album, a new life. You can buy a bus, go on the road, do a tour of Europe! Just kidding, or am I?

It was extremely exciting for me to know that I did not have to live by and continue to use my family's crazy thoughts, opinions, mindsets, and beliefs. I can form my own opinions, follow my own rules, and create my own crazy thoughts and beliefs.

No longer do I blame my family for living in the past or use those past hurts as excuses to be miserable. I don't complain about how they "done me wrong" or how my life would have been so different if only I had more guidance, support, money, and a better family blah, blah, blah.

The more I learned about myself, the fewer excuses I had for continuing to live my life with unhappiness and self-loathing. I understood why I had become that person. The knowledge of the subjects I have learned and take claim to have learned creates a responsibility clause within my subconscious mind of that said knowledge. Remember, it is your responsibility to believe in yourself, and your mission (if you choose to accept it) is to discover who you want to become.

It would be easy to say, "That sounds like a lot of work." And it can be. When I reached my lowest point, I decided to do the work because I discovered that my life is beautiful, fun, and full of adventures. I am transparent. I am not afraid to try new things, meet various kinds of people, and appreciate them for who they are, not the version I think they should be.

_____

_____

_____

_____

_____

_____

_____

_____

_____

_____

_____

# How To Forgive Anyone

Of course, there is contrast, and there will always be something happening to disrupt the norm in your life. Sometimes, interruptions can make it difficult to stay happy and positive, and sometimes, it can be the greatest thing ever. With the right attitude, nothing can bring you down for very long.

If your life is not your own, then it belongs to someone else. I wanted to create a life of wonder, and when contrast would show up, I would look at it and decide how to react to it. My reactions to anything are how I figure out how long that contrast will affect me. It's my choice. It's your choice.

I hope you get to know the power that comes from changing your mindsets and what you believe in. What you believe in today is not what you have to believe in tomorrow. Choosing your own mindset will be unique only to you. The only rules to follow are your rules. No one else will be allowed to tell you what will or will not make your life happy. This is enormously powerful knowledge when it comes to changing what you want to change about yourself.

How do you change your mindsets? There are a couple of techniques I swear by, such as hypnosis and affirmations. Hypnosis is life-affirming. It has the ability to rewire your subconscious mind and impress upon it what you want to change. I used hypnosis for confidence building, removing my poverty mentality, weight loss, stress, anxiety, and motivation.

It was so effective for me that I now have a Master's in Hypnotherapy. I love helping people change a part of them almost instantly. It can help you through trauma, remove fears and phobias, alleviate addictions, and so much more. I highly recommend this for anyone trying to change, forget, or improve. It works!

The other favorite mindset changer is using affirmations. They are so effective. When repeated throughout your day, they affirm your conscious mind, and your conscious mind will order your subconscious mind that is what you want to believe in.

### These Are A Few Of My Favorites:

*Every day and in every way,
my life is always working out for me.*

*Every day and in every way,
i remember to stay in the present moment.*

*Every day and in every way,
money naturally flows to me.*

*Every day and in every way,
my body is always healing itself.*

Louise Hay, who founded Hay House (www.hayhouse.com) has transformed so many people's lives with her books, podcasts, and radio shows. She is the one who taught us the importance of affirmations for all of us to reclaim our power and change our lives. She wrote:

"In the infinity of life where I am,
all is perfect, whole, and complete.
I see any resistance patterns within me,
only as something else to release.
They have no power over me.
I am the power in my world.
I flow with the changes taking place in my
life as best I can.
I approve of myself and the way I am changing.
I am doing the best I can.
Each day gets easier.
I rejoice that I am in the rhythm
and flow of my ever-changing life.
Today is a wonderful day.
I choose to make it so.
All is well in my world."

"Refuse to cater to low-energy mental activity. Be determined to unquestionably place your thoughts not on what you can't do but on what you intend to create."

- Dr. Wayne Dyer

"Because of the way you have been thinking, you have convinced your body of these things. As you change your thinking, you will change the thinking of the cells of your body as well. The cells of your body are so compliant to what is going on with your thoughts."

-Abraham-Hicks

## Chapter 4:
## Your Thoughts Create Your Reality

It took reading several different books before I understood what "thoughts create your reality" meant. Understanding the power of your thoughts will literally change your life. Whatever you think about will come to you. I have evaluated and assessed this theory many times, and it works very well.

Whenever a situation would happen to me that I thought I did not ask for, I would backtrack my thoughts and realize, yes, I did make that happen. I was thinking about what I DID NOT want to happen. I had put so many feelings into not wanting this that my subconscious mind (it doesn't know the difference between what is or isn't real) gave me what I was feeling.

Albert Einstein said, "When something vibrates, the electron from the universe resonates with it. Everything is connected. Energy cannot be created or destroyed; it can only be changed from one form to another." Everything is energy.

The world runs on vibrational frequencies, and our thoughts are no exception. When you think a thought and focus on that thought for more than seventeen seconds, as Abraham Hicks explains, you activate a matching vibration in the quantum field. When you add an emotional attachment to that thought, the more powerful that vibration becomes. And the universe must comply with what you are thinking. That is the universal law called "THE LAW OF ATTRACTION."

This is not just woo-woo stuff; this has been proven through studies for years. Quantum physics, the quantum field, and the law of attraction have been written about in tons of books. My favorite is "Breaking the Habit of Being Yourself" by Dr. Joe Dispenza. Impressive read! It helped me with my transition to finding a new me. It's easy to understand. Also, "E-Squared" by Pam Grout contains nine do-it-yourself experiments that prove "your thoughts create your reality." Great fun book!

Our conscious mind and our subconscious mind have two distinct aspects to them. Our conscious mind is where our decisions are formed. It is the reasoning mind. For example, you choose where to live, what to think about, if you should go dancing tonight or stay home and watch the movie *"King Kong vs. Godzilla."* It is your choice. That's a conscious decision.

Have you heard the saying, "We only use 10% of our brain"? Well, that's true, but what most people don't know is that the other 90% is controlled by our subconscious mind. It controls our heartbeat and our organs; basically, everything in our body is controlled by our subconscious mind. Our memories and emotional trauma dramas are kept safe; our habits, good or bad, are also controlled by our subconscious mind.

It will remind us of how good it felt to smoke a cigarette when we were sad, upset, or had a satisfying meal. We reached for a smoke and were looking for some kind of satisfaction. Same thing for any kind of drug; if that drug made you feel good when you were not feeling good, then your subconscious mind is doing what it is supposed to do: reminding you what it is that makes you feel good, not realizing that it was a bad habit, but that it made you feel good. I hope this is making sense. That is why it was so hard for some to quit, because of the emotional attachment we had to that cigarette or drug.

You use your conscious mind when you're awake, and it sleeps when you do. Your subconscious mind never sleeps. While you're awake, you think and think and think. Did you know that 98% of people have the same thoughts today as they did yesterday? What are some repetitive thoughts you have?

## Give This A Try:

Observe your thoughts. What have you been thinking about lately? Who are you thinking about? Are you thinking the same thoughts every day? How many times a day? What triggers specific thoughts? Write down any thoughts that you catch yourself repeating. It may surprise you what they are and what triggered you to have that thought.

_____

_____

_____

_____

_____

_____

_____

_____

_____

_____

If you have never heard this information before, I understand it's a lot of info to take in, but please stay with me; it will be worth it!

Thinking positive thoughts can improve brain function. It is not natural to be unhappy; it is only natural to be happy. There are so many other books that inspired me to change, and I want to tell you about all of them, but that would be a little crazy to do. I listed them in the back of the book. I hope they resonate with what you want to achieve.

Are you sensing a theme here? Yes, you are correct; it is changing the way you think, feel, and do everything in your life. This may be daunting to think about (pun intended), but life is about expansion and growing through our challenges and diversities. These are what make us great human beings.

Most people bitch and complain about their life's dramas instead of looking to embrace the contrast, which I know is hard to understand, the difficulty of embracing what makes us hurt. I have learned that the life you choose to live is the life you will have. So, instead of complaining, try to turn your thoughts into questions about what just happened. Ask yourself, what can I learn from that experience? You may be surprised to learn something new about yourself.

Here is a trick I do when I can't seem to get the negative thoughts out of my head: I want to change instantly how I feel. I love puppies. So, I imagine I am on the floor surrounded by eleven four-week-old puppies. They are tackling and giving me puppy kisses; I am in puppy heaven.

Close your eyes for a couple of minutes and feel the love of these sweet animals. It does not have to be puppies; use any small animal that you love. Go ahead, they will not hurt you.

You are smiling. How can you not be smiling? They are pure, unconditional love. You were in the present moment, focusing on what was happening and visualizing something special, and for that moment, you forgot about that memory from your past. Whenever you start to relive a not-so-good memory, try this trick.

Close your eyes again and visualize those ten sweet babies giving you tons of kisses. Or if there is something else that makes you smile every time you think of it, write it down. Writing a happy thought down helps impress upon your subconscious mind this happy feeling. It's the same as anchoring that confident feeling we did in Chapter 2.

_____

_____

_____

_____

_____

_____

_____

_____

## Chapter 5:
## *Living In The Present Moment*

"Most people treat the present moment as if it were an obstacle they need to overcome. Since the present moment is life itself, it is an insane way to live."

-Eckhart Tolle

"Observe the many ways in which unease, discontent, and tension arise within you through unnecessary judgment, resistance to what is, and denial of the Now."

-Eckhart Tolle

The more attention you place on your past, the more energy you feed it. Give attention to the present moment. Give attention to your behavior, your reactions, your moods, your thoughts, your emotions, your fears, and desires as they occur in the present.

You cannot find yourself in the past. Eckhart Tolle says, "If you can be present enough to watch all those things without being critical or analytical, even nonjudgmental, then you are dealing with the past and dissolving it through the power of your presence. You find yourself by coming into the presence."

Everyone has an inner being. I believe you could call it your soul, conscience, inner gut, or even better half. I have learned to trust my intuition and listen to what it has to say. Can you remember a time when you listened to your intuition, and a good thing happened because of it? Can you remember a time when you did not listen to that gut feeling, and a terrible thing happened because of it? If you're up to it, write down those memories.

_____

_____

_____

_____

_____

_____

_____

_____

_____

_____

## No one is you, and that is your power!

I am so proud of what I discovered about myself so far. I have changed. I have evolved. I have become happier than I ever remember being. But too often, I still had those sad, bad, negative memories that would surface. That is expected, especially if you have been through a surmountable amount of pain. I found myself identifying with other people who had the same sad stories I did, and I would fall back into my old, depressed self.

Once I recognized those negative thoughts, I would, as fast as possible, rethink my thoughts back to where they should be, on the happier side of my life. Still, it seems after all the self-educating I have done, I kept having this recurring feeling that I needed to do more for myself. I still felt like I was carrying around this weight. I felt I should be flying light as a feather from all the knowledge and acceptance I have gained. It was a feeling I could not shake.

One day, while I was meditating, I asked my angels what this feeling of heavy weight I was still carrying was. I felt in my spiritual awakening process that I must have missed something. There was still a part of me I needed to release, something important. After a few moments of silence, I heard an angelic voice say,

*It is through forgiveness that you will find inner peace*

That was an impressive answer! I thought that shouldn't be too hard, right? People have been forgiving each other for hundreds of years. Well, unfortunately, eighty percent of what I found was religion-based. I have never been a religious girl. Do I believe in God? Yes. Do I believe in religion? No.

I grew up in a "cult-like" religion where if you did not believe or live in the way that you were told to believe or live, then you were a sinner. It never made sense to me; I rebelled, and I questioned their beliefs. They did not appreciate that! I ended up being disfellowshipped, which meant during the church meetings, I had to sit in the last row in the back of the church, and no one was allowed to talk to me. Really??

Because I'm sure if Jesus had shown up, he would have sat right next to me and asked how I was doing. Because if I were a religious person, I would consider unconditional love instead of threats and judgment. Anyway, I did not want this to be about God; I just wanted to forgive my past pains and move on.

_____

_____

_____

_____

_____

_____

_____

_____

_____

_____

Before I had forgiven anyone, whenever I had encountered one of the people from my past who hurt me, my reaction was anything but calm. My heart would be racing, my hands would start sweating, and the voice in my head would be yelling, "PLEASE GOD, NOT TODAY."

You already know how I feel about confrontation! I do not want to pretend to like this person! I do not want to be nice to this person! This person hurt me! I just wanted to run the other way. That is how I reacted before forgiving; then everything changed.

Once I forgave "those people," my reaction to them was so different. I noticed my heart was not racing, no hand sweating; it was like meeting that person prior to the pain they inflicted on me. It was just wonderful. It is such a peaceful feeling, being detached from the emotions that used to consume me before forgiving them. I loved that I did not give a rat's patootie about what they thought of me!

One of the best parts of forgiving someone is that you become nonjudgmental of who they are; you have a strong, confident, powerful feeling that fills your whole body! If you must have a conversation with a "past pain" person after forgiving them, it will be okay because you are in control.

Just smile because it is an exhilarating feeling; enjoy this; it is like you are in a dream state. You can hear them talking, not really caring what they are saying because your mind is singing, "This person has no idea that I have forgiven them, and they never will."

Robyn Iona

Silently remind yourself that you are on a more positive, happiness path. While looking at them in the eye, silently say, "You have not a clue that no matter what you say, I will never allow you to hurt me again or take my power away." Just smile and nod your head, excuse yourself, and turn away with a swagger in your walk and your beautiful head held high.

A few years later, after forgiving those people, I went to a funeral for an ex-boyfriend who had recently died of cancer way too young. As I entered the building, I was not even thinking about who might come to the service; in fact, I had not even thought about any of those people in forever. Some of the people who had attended this memorial were from my past. In fact, I counted seven people who were on my list that I had forgiven. But I did not realize this until much later.

I said hello and started giving out hugs like they were candy, as I usually do. Once I found my seat, I started to look around. Do you know when that light bulb over your head lights up when you think about a great idea or remember an important thing? Well, my light bulb turned into a turbo spotlight! I could not believe it!

_____

_____

_____

_____

_____

_____

I yelled in my head, "Oh my freaking God," because I had totally forgotten about the pain these people had inflicted on me! There was absolutely not one part of me that was uncomfortable while I was saying hello or hugging these "past pains." It was incredible! I was so excited and so happy that my forgiveness process worked! What a relief to know that the pain they caused was not affecting me and that pain was gone forever!

"The only thing that is ultimately real about your journey is the step you are taking at this very moment. that's all there is."

-Eckhart Tolle

## Chapter 6:
## The Act Of Forgiving Yourself

In Hinduism, Namaste translates to "the divine in me bows to the divine in you." This creates vibrations and a loop of bliss to pass positive energy on to the one receiving the gesture. The reason I have you saying this after each statement is because this word has a strong frequency of love, which is exactly what you want while forgiving yourself and others.

Please read this formula beforehand so you will know what to expect. Schedule a couple of hours of "you" time. You must be alone; lock the doors for privacy. Please make sure you have no distractions. This is to be taken seriously and needs your undivided attention.

After reading Part One, reread it again, but this time, record it on your phone. This process works best if you say the words OUT LOUD, and recording them beforehand will make the process easier and more effective. Visualizing the words you are saying has a profound impact on your results; just keep your eyes closed and let your imagination do its thing.

OPTIONAL:

- Light a candle.

- Burn sandalwood or sage incense.

- If you have a clear and/or pink quartz crystal, place it close to you.

- Have a glass of water nearby.

Forgiving yourself creates an amazing feeling, and if you feel the need to cry afterward, then please allow yourself to let it go. This bears repeating: crying is an emotion that needs to be expressed. The tears are not from being sad or happy. Your body is releasing those repressed emotions you have held onto for who knows how long.

Letting go of all those pent-up emotions can be the most cleansing feeling you may ever know. Your face may look funny, all wet and puffy; your eyes may get a little red, but just for a little while. Allowing that feeling of release, "closely resembling a great, intense orgasm," ha-ha, made you smile! It will be well worth it to just let go!

Start recording here:

Get comfortable, close your eyes, take a deep breath in... hold for the (count of three)... slowly exhale... again... deep breath in... hold for the (count of three)... slowly exhale... one more time... deep breath in... hold (count of three)... slowly exhale... now relax and breathe normally.

Place your palms together and put them in front of your heart.

Imagine a luminous multicolored light pouring from the heavens, as soft as a cloud and smooth as black velvet. This wonderful light is warm as it gently pours over your head... your face... your neck... Can you feel it hold you so tenderly... as this white light covers your shoulders... your arms... your chest... your back...

Can you feel the warmth of this beautiful light that is now flowing down over your belly... your lower back... your hips... You feel safe... as this beautiful light cascades down your thighs... your knees... your feet... Now, your whole body, every cell, every atom inside you, is filled with this white illuminating energy.

You are at peace. You feel a loving light inside your heart; this positive light will be with you to provide comfort while forgiving yourself.

Take a deep breath and exhale slowly. Now, just breathe normally and relax for a minute. Enjoy this wonderful feeling of being surrounded by love and beautiful white light.

When you're ready, picture yourself sitting on a bench; this bench is in the middle of a beautiful park. You see the tops of the majestic snow-capped mountains kissing the blue skies. You smell the aroma of pine trees as they embrace the clear and calm lake that is in front of you. It is a perfectly perfect day as the light breeze carries the scent of lilac bushes blooming nearby. You feel the warmth of the sun as it softly caresses your face. You take a deep breath in and slowly exhale all your worries away.

Do you remember when you were a young child, age 6 or 7? What was your favorite thing to do? Play hopscotch? Make mud pies? Ride your bike around the neighborhood? Play with your brothers and sisters? Play with your neighborhood friends?

What did you look like? Were you long and lanky? Were you tiny and petite? Were you the thick, strong kid on the block? Remember the details: were you missing any teeth? What color was your hair? Did you have a buzz cut or long, wavy hair? Hold this picture of you as a kid.

While you are resting on this bench in this beautiful park, with your eyes still closed, you remember what you looked like when you were young and innocent, when life was fun and full of mystery, when you believed that anything was possible.

As your mind is wandering to that time in your life, you hear a small child's voice: it is coming from the woods. You hear it again; you hear your name being called by this child.

Using your creative imagination while keeping your eyes closed, you look up and see this young child running towards you. This child calls out your name again, and as the child is getting closer, you begin to recognize this child; you are amazed that this child looks just like you did when you were a kid. This child is YOU! The child running towards you is smiling and so happy to see you. You see that his/her arms are wide open, in the "I am ready" hugging position. So, you reciprocate and reach out with your arms wide open to embrace this child that is YOU.

You both hug each other; this is a real hug, the kind of hug that only an innocent child can give to someone whom they love unconditionally. Feel how wonderful this LOVE is for yourself while you are hugging this child that is you. Relax into each other's arms, hold that hug as long as you can; there is no hurry. Just an uncomplicated, unconditional moment in time.

It is important to say your name aloud because it confirms and imprints to your subconscious mind what you are feeling about forgiving yourself.

Keep hugging the younger you and, from your pre-recorded recording, say OUT LOUD:

1. (Your Name),

*The Child Of Unconditional Love Within Me Recognizes The Child Of Unconditional Love Within This Older Version Of Myself.*

                                                                     Namaste.

2. (Your Name),

*I Forgive Myself For Anything I May Have Done To Hurt Myself Or Anyone From My Past.*

                                                                      Namaste.

3. (Your Name),

*I Forgive Myself For Holding On To The Pain From My Past.*

                                                                      Namaste.

4. (Your Name),

*I Understand That It Is My Responsibility To Be Happy.*

                                                                      Namaste.

5. (Your Name),

   *I Openly Choose To Find Love Within Myself, And I Openly Choose To Receive Love.*

   *Namaste.*

6. (Your Name),

   *I Am Worthy Of All Things That Make Me Happy. I Am Worthy Of All Things That Make Me Happy. I Am Worthy Of All Things That Make Me Happy.*

   *Namaste.*

7. (Your Name),

   *What Happened Yesterday Can Never Be Changed, And I Accept This.*

   *Namaste.*

8. (Your Name),

   *I Will No Longer Be Controlled By My Past. I Will Remember To Stay In The Present Moment.*

   *Namaste.*

9. (Your Name),

   *I Will Embrace My Inner Child And Learn How To Play Again.*

   *Namaste.*

Now feel the younger you releasing from your warm embrace, kissing your cheek, and whispering, "You got this!" Then, the child turns away and skips into the sunshine.

Stop recording.

Take a moment and be aware of how you are emotionally feeling. Know that it is OKAY to cry if you feel the need. I cried a lot after forgiving myself. I was unsure why, but I knew I had to let that emotion go, and this was a perfect time to do it. I remember once I stopped crying, I started to laugh because it felt so wonderful to let go.

Remember, YOU are not doing this to impress anyone but yourself. YOU are not doing this to make anyone else happy. YOU are not doing this because "it's the nice thing to do." YOU are only doing this to make YOU happy, to acknowledge YOUR happiness.

Today, YOU gave yourself permission to forgive yourself. Be proud of yourself; YOU totally deserve this!

A truly great person never loses the openness of a child.

Some of you will find it hard to forgive yourself, maybe because someone convinced you that "you were not worth it" or said things when you were a child that made you believe that you weren't important enough to love.

A method I used to work through this worked for me tremendously. I learned it from a book called "Mirror Work" written by Louise Hay. The condensed version is: you look into a mirror and stare into your eyes. Looking closely, notice the colors; what shape are they? Keep looking, and as you continue to look deep into your eyes, say aloud, "(Your name), I love you."

People will react according to their opinion of themselves. Most of us will have a challenging time doing this. Can you do it on the first try without pulling away? I could not; in fact, I cried every time I tried. It took me months to be able to say "I love you" to my eyes without crying.

I was determined to learn to LOVE MYSELF! So, I made myself say "I love you" to me every morning before putting on my makeup. I cried a lot, but it did get easier and easier until, finally, it happened.

I could look into my beautiful blue eyes and say the words, "I LOVE YOU, ROBYN!" Whew, it took a long while, but it was well worth it. Now I can say it without crying. Try it yourself; write down the date that you start and see how long it takes you to say it with unconditional love.

_____

_____

_____

_____

_____

_____

_____

_____

_____

_____

_____

_____

_____

_____

"We are what we think about. all that we are arises with our thoughts. with our thoughts, we make our world."

-Buddha

*You weren't born knowing who you are. your life experiences are your lessons learned. these life lessons have created who you have become. the wisdom you have gained is used to make your life better and to inspire others.*

-Iona

*You are the only thinker in your universe!*

*Confidence is more powerful than fear!*

## Things I Am No Longer Apologizing For:

- My feelings!
- Asking for clarity when I don't understand!
- Having firm boundaries!
- Saying "no" to something I don't want to do!
- Being emotional or crying!
- Not answering my phone when I don't want to or can't!
- Needing to take a break!
- How other people behave!
- Changing and becoming better!
- Not agreeing with someone!
- Putting myself first; I can't be anything to anyone if I am nothing to myself!
- Not settling for less than I deserve!
- Letting go when I need to!
- Healing at my own pace!
- Meditating!
- Changing my career!
- Laughing out loud!

- Not finishing a project!
- Not caring what others think of me!
- Being kind to strangers!
- Going shopping all day long!
- Keeping my secrets!
- If someone doesn't get me!

Can you think of anything for which you will no longer apologize?

_____

_____

_____

_____

_____

_____

_____

_____

_____

_____

_____

_____

_____

_____

_____

_____

## Chapter 7:
## *Taking Responsibility For Your Happiness*

Being mindful of the importance of forgiveness can give you greater clarification and understanding of your inner being. The wisdom I gained through forgiveness while pursuing illumination goes far beyond anything I imagined.

My ability to forgive became my extraordinary evolutionary path to enlightenment. It created a new level for me to love and have more compassion and understanding. Depending on the complexity and how deep your mental anguish is, the emotional attachments you have to that pain will determine if you will need to forgive this person more than once. You will naturally become aware of which memory will need more attention and which ones will not.

If, after you forgive a person, you find yourself still reliving a past pain, it is okay. This is because you have not completely let it go and still identify with it. It is normal to have those big pains resurface. These are people who have caused major, traumatic, hurtful, and uncomfortable circumstances. That pain has been part of who you are now, and sadly, some events have stayed with you for many years.

The resurfacing of your past pain is part of your healing process. When you begin to feel pain from memory, close your eyes and acknowledge that this happened to you. Cry a little if you can cry from deep inside yourself. Once you stop, blow your nose and take a deep breath. Cry again if you need to; you are releasing emotions that no longer serve you, and know that everything will be okay!

By releasing and letting go of your past pains, you are surrendering that past pain to the universe, allowing yourself to be free of that pain. The more you let go, the more your subconscious mind will allow other pains to show themselves. Yes, I know this may suck, remembering your past, but if you're serious about NOT living in your past, then this must take place. Trust that it will be worth it! This, too, is a wonderful thing.

As you release those memories through this forgiveness process, you will begin to feel lighter and sleep better. Also, remember you are not those memories; they may have been a part of your everyday life before today, but now you are letting them go and permitting yourself to heal from them.

Do the forgiveness process again for someone who keeps resurfacing in your thoughts. I had to forgive my mother frequently because I had several incidents that I had forgotten about. These were locked away deep within my subconscious, and when they resurfaced, I needed to forgive her again.

Imagine what your life would look like if you did not waste all those hours thinking of past pains or if you could have done something different. You cannot go back and change it, and better yet, they cannot hurt you anymore (unless you allow them to). However, since you are reading this book, you are learning how you will not let them hurt you again.

You know better now, and you have the confidence and wisdom to remember you are in control of your thoughts. Your thoughts give you power; your thoughts, as you know them, create your reality.

Your state of mind is most important before doing this process of forgiving. You must really WANT to forgive yourself and "that person." This means you are ready to let go of what "that person" had inflicted on you. You are ready to learn how important and special you are to this world; the talents and gifts that you share are what make this world a better place to live. We humans need you to forgive your past so we can see who you really are, so YOU can see who you really are.

Please remember that what "that person" did to you is not okay! And they are not getting away with it; it just means you are taking your power back, and THEY NO LONGER HAVE CONTROL over you. If it helps, please remember NO ONE WAS BORN TO HURT ANYONE! We are born perfectly innocent to life, and then life changes everything.

Forgiving does not mean forgetting. This is not about "them." It is about YOU, healing from their actions. This is your reaction to the pain that was given to you. It is that simple! So, you got this: belief, trust, and know it is the opportunity to finally realize:

*You can not change the past, but you can release it.*

*Until you accept what is, you cannot move into what might be.*

*-Buddha*

## Chapter 8:
## *The Act Of Forgiving Those "Past Pains"*

When you are ready, make a list of all the people you are going to forgive. Look back at your childhood. parents, stepparents, grandparents, brothers, sisters, aunts, uncles, cousins, students from grade school, high school, college, teachers, girlfriends, boyfriends, husbands, wives, lovers, one-night stands, roommates, partners, bosses, business associates, co-workers, anyone at any time in your life who has hurt you and needs forgiving. Take your time; my list was long, 57 people is extremely painful, and it took several days to complete.

Remember, for the most effective results, read this formula beforehand and record it on your phone. So you will know what to expect. Schedule a couple of hours of "you" time. You must be alone; lock the doors for privacy. Please make sure you have no distractions. This is to be taken seriously and needs your undivided attention.

SET-UP...

Read this first, then record it before continuing:

OPTIONAL:

- Light a candle.

- Hold a rose or clear quartz crystal for calmness, if possible.

- Glass of water

Pick a person from your list; try one of your fender benders from your bag that hurts. This means choosing a person on a scale of one to ten, ten being the most hurtful, and maybe choosing a three or four for the first time. This is because when you forgive the biggest ones, you will have more confidence and practice in the forgiveness process.

You will need two chairs facing each other; make one chair comfortable and the other not so comfortable. As you sit in your comfy chair, imagine that the person you are forgiving is sitting across from you. If you want, you can place duct tape over their mouth, just in case you think they might talk. Dress them up as you see fit, but stay in a positive, loving state; this is for you, not them.

Read this first, then record it before continuing:

Get comfortable, close your eyes, take a deep breath in... hold for the (count of three)... slowly exhale... again... deep breath in... hold for (count of three)... one more time, deep breath in... hold... exhale slowly.

With eyes closed...

Imagine a luminous multicolored light pouring from the heavens, as soft as a cloud and smooth as black velvet... This light is warm and transparent; you begin to feel it gently, slowly pour over your head... your face... your neck... Can you feel it hold you so tenderly... as this white light covers your shoulders... your arms... your chest... your back...

Can you feel the warmth of this beautiful light that is now flowing down over your belly... your lower back... your hips... You can feel safe... as this beautiful light encompasses your thighs... your knees... your feet... now it's covering your whole body; every cell... every atom... in your physical body has now absorbed this white illuminating energy.

Take a deep breath in... hold (count of three)... slowly exhale... another deep breath in... hold (count of three)... slowly exhale... one last time, deep breath in... hold (count of three)... slowly exhale... now relax and breathe normally.

Now imagine "that person" sitting in the chair across from you. You can imagine them as they looked at the time they hurt you. Remind them of what they did to you; tell them how it has affected your life. Tell them that because of them, you are having issues with...! Say, "Today, I am taking my power back; you will not be able to hurt me again!"

The (Name) reference is the name of the person you are forgiving.

Say these words out loud while listening to your recorded version.

1. (Name),

    *The inner being within me recognizes the inner being within you.*

    Namaste.

2. (Name),

    *Love's presence within me recognizes love's presence within you.*

    Namaste.

3. (Name),

    *The child of unconditional love within me recognizes the child of unconditional love within you.*

    Namaste.

4. (Name),

    *I am aware my past has brought me to this moment of clarity, and because of you, i know what i want, and i know what i don't want.*

    Namaste.

5. (Name),

    *I have acknowledged my past and have released it. may you acknowledge your past and release it.*

    Namaste.

6. (Name),

*I have made the choice to no longer allow you to hurt me. may you no longer hurt anyone else.*

                                                      Namaste.

Take a deep breath, INHALING the white light that surrounds you, and then exhale slowly and relax your muscles as you do so.

Now, visualize that the person across from you is changing its form. With your mind's eye, you see that their physical body is transforming, slowly dissolving, changing; you see that human body being consumed, being surrounded by little orbs of white light; these magnificent lights are swirling all around the body, like a little tornado of effervescent bubbles.

It is magical and mystical, as you are watching all these little lights swirl around faster and faster until you no longer see a physical body. You realize the body is no longer there because it has transformed into a beautiful orb; all those little lights come together and form a softball-sized ball. This orb is now floating above the chair where that person was previously sitting.

You are now speaking to this person on a spiritual level.

Listening to your pre-recorded version, remember to say everything OUT LOUD.

1. (Name),

*I know see you as a spiritual being. it is only love I see. may the spiritual being within you change how you see love.*

                                                      Namaste.

2. (Name),

*I have spiritually grown and evolved. may you spiritually grow and evolve.*

Namaste.

3. (Name),

*As I expand my human experience, I choose to release you from my thoughts. I cut all inappropriate and unauthorized cords attached to me from you.*

Namaste.

4. (Name),

*Blessings be to me. Blessings be to you.*

Namaste.

5. (Name),

*I now take back my power and will be true to myself. may you see the power of love within you and find your true self.*

Namaste.

6. (Name),

*I have acknowledged that you were my teacher through conflict, contrast, and pain. I have accepted this as growth.*

Namaste.

7. (Name),

*May you acknowledge the pain, conflict, and contrast you have given me and find growth within this knowledge.*

Namaste.

8. (Name),

*May love and peace be with me. May love and peace be with you.*

Namaste.

9. (Name),

*I am blessed with inner healing and spiritual maturity. I bless you with inner healing and spiritual maturity.*

Namaste.

10. (Name),

*Go in peace. Go in love.*

Namaste.

11. *I completely release you. **(name)**, I completely release you. **(name)**, I completely release you. **(name)**,*

Namaste.

12. (Name),

*You are completely forgiven. **(name)**, You are completely forgiven. **(name)**, You are completely forgiven. **(name)**,*

Namaste

13. (Name),

*I release you into the light and let love be with you always. **(name)**, I release you into the light and let love be with you always. **(name)**, I release you into the light and let love be with you always.*

Namaste.

As you look at the floating orb, you feel love inside you; complete, unconditional, pure love fills your body as this orb radiates pure white light. Your body is absorbing this pure love. You see that the light from the orb is starting to grow brighter, and it begins to rise. This light fills the room with iridescent colors.

This spiritual being is rising higher and higher. You watch as it floats upwards to the ceiling, and all at once, like the blink of an eye, it disappears, and the orb and the light have vanished. Poof! The room is clear, and you will not allow yourself to be hurt by this person again.

That "past pain" has now left the building, and it is no longer part of you. Remember this feeling; do not think of anything for a moment, and breathe in this feeling of letting go. You are free. Congratulations...

Yesterday Is Gone,
Tomorrow Is A Mystery,
Today Is A Gift,
That Is Why It Is Called
The Present

....

Robyn Iona

Electricity Is A Name We Give An Invisible Power
We Do Not Fully Comprehend!

We Can Not See Life,
Yet We Know We Are Alive.

## Chapter 9:
## Giving Yourself Permission To Let Go

Contrast is what makes us grow as human beings. I think we all have heard someone say, "I hate change." People like it when things in their lives stay the same. But it never does, does it? Life is always changing, and it always will be. You cannot stop it. The seasons change every year; you always know that spring, summer, winter, and fall will always happen, but the scenery is always changing.

This is exactly what makes the human experience great: we get to choose what to believe in, where to go or not go, learn or not learn, and be or not be whatever we choose. People will be who they are; I believe no one is better than anyone else. I think we are at distinct levels of learning who we are and where we came from.

As you know by now, it took me years to learn to embrace change, realizing that my life, my situations, and the people around me would always be different. I found new confidence in going beyond my comfort zone because I expected it to change, even if it felt uncomfortable.

Do you know people who are always worried about the *"what ifs"* in their life situations? *What if he/she doesn't like me? What if the plane crashes? What if I get a hole in my stocking? What if they really like me?*

You get the picture.

Fear is everywhere!

Be it TV commercials or the ads that pop up on your phone. So it's important that you stay in the present moment and continue to embrace the new you.

"F-E-A-R

Has Two Meanings:

Forget Everything

And Run Or Face Everything

And Rise.

The Choice Is Yours."

-Zig Ziglar

Can you think of any fears that may be holding you back?

You cannot change the way people will react to any given situation, but you can be aware of how you react. When you react in a negative or unpleasant way, you will get more uncomfortable.

The next time a negative situation arises, review your actions; you may be surprised at your findings. I know I was.

I used to be a "people pleaser." I still am to a degree, but on my own terms. There is nothing wrong with helping people and being nice; I am always smiling at strangers, saying hello for no other reason. I love being happy, and I don't care if it bothers people because my motto is:

It's none of my business

What you think of me,

It's what i think of

Me that matters.

I remember how I felt after I had finished forgiving my fifty-seven people. It took seven full days to finish, and I did it! Every day, it was easier to forgive the next person on my list. Every night, I slept better than the night before. Every morning, I would wake up with a smile on my face. IT IS IMPRESSIVE!

I felt so free, like a weight had been lifted off my body. I was proud of myself. At that time, I did not know if the forgiveness process worked, but I knew that something in me had changed.

I did know there was a happy, fuzzy feeling inside my heart. I felt excited about what I didn't know. I just knew that forgiving those past pains was the best thing I could have ever done for my sanity, my future, or, in simple terms, just for me. I felt like I could rule the world—not really rule the world, just be the queen of my own world.

It has been a habit to think of those people. I do not know how long you have been thinking of your situation, but I have had the same thoughts for years: different people who committed different crimes against me, different days when the memories would pop back into my head.

When that does happen, and it will happen, you will need a reminder that says, "Oh, that's right. I have forgiven you, and I took back my power. And I released you from my thoughts." Change the subject in your head to anything that is around you, wherever you are. Just find a distraction. It works 99% of the time!

_____

_____

_____

## How To Forgive Anyone

Figure out what works best for you, whether you make big signs all over your house reminding you that you released those emotional attachments or small affirmations written in inconspicuous places reminding you that you are the only one who is in control of your thoughts.

For me, small affirmations were placed everywhere, not just a reminder that I had forgiven someone, but to affirm that I was going in a different direction that I decided and made a choice to move on to a happier life without the thought of them.

When you come across someone that you have forgiven, remember they do not know what you did. They do not know that your life is becoming better and better. Please do not tell them. I mean, of course, you can if you want to. But how fun is it to look at them knowing that you are a different person now? Depending on how long it will be before you may run into one you have forgiven will decide how you react when you are face to face with them. Just be cool if it is soon after. You have this! Remember:

You have taken your power away from them; they will never hurt you again because you will not let them. In time, as I did, you may learn that you will have more compassion for them. You will look at them differently; instead of the pain you used to feel, now feel grateful for the part they played in your life.

# How To Forgive Anyone

_____
_____
_____
_____
_____
_____
_____
_____
_____
_____
_____
_____
_____
_____
_____
_____
_____
_____
_____
_____
_____

Because of them, you are more confident; you have better clarity about who you are now. Because of them, you know what you do want and what you don't want. They are in a different place than you are now. And that is the way you want it to be. Let them live the life they have chosen, and you live the life you were born to live.

> The best weight loss
>
> You will ever lose
>
> Is the weight you lose
>
> When you let go
>
> Of your past pains...

I say this again: Your words have great power because they come from your thoughts. Your thoughts create your reality. The Law of Attraction is the law of the universe. When we have contrast or uncomfortable situations in our lives, we expand. We need that contrast to learn what we do want and what we don't want.

If you have not heard of this before, look up Abraham Hicks on YouTube and watch one of the countless teaching videos. For me, Abraham Hicks and all my years of research gave me even more clarity.

No one can read your thoughts. You are the only one in control of them. Your thoughts are really the only, for sure thing in your life that YOU CAN CONTROL AND CHANGE.

That is your power; your thoughts are only yours, and no one can think for you. No one else can keep you from thinking any thought you want to think. I loved learning that; it gave me the confidence to be anyone or anywhere I wanted with just my thoughts.

When you criticize yourself or blame anything or anybody, notice how you are feeling. Whenever you feel bad inside, it is your indicator that you are thinking negatively. Once you are aware of the negative thoughts, then be a self-observer. Replay the situation, watch your reactions, then play it back and see what it looks like with a more positive spin on it. Remember, you will never feel good when having negative feelings.

No one is destined to live a life of unhappiness, poverty, or without love because each of us has the ability to change everything in this life. Every person has their own unique circumstances to overcome, but every single person has the opportunity to achieve anything that will make them happy.

I may not personally know you, but I want to say I am proud of you. I am proud because you care enough about yourself to care how you feel. Feeling good is what you want most of all. It is the only thing that will bring you what you want; staying in a happy state of mind brings you a happy life.

I understand that it is hard to let go of what has become a "norm" for many of you. I know; I, too, clung to what was familiar to me. You have had a lot of unpleasant baggage from your past, and when you look back, you think, "How the hell did I ever survive that?" But you did, and you are here reading this book, making it better. My wish is that you will find a new norm.

Sometimes, when we do not have the courage to change the things we want to, life (the universe) will change those things for us while directing us to a new path. No matter how hard someone can try, you cannot stop growing and evolving; that is what living is all about.

Every positive step that you take

Is transforming your being.

With the consistent use of your will

And steady, determined practice of what you have learned,

You will be amazed at how fast transformation will take place.

Transformation of your being

Brings a peace and a joy

That is indescribable.

You have to experience it to know it,

And once you do,

You will never go back.

-The Secret

# *Acknowledgments*

I would like to acknowledge and thank all the authors and their books for inspiring me to become the person I am today:

- *The Secret* by Rhonda Byrne
- *The Power of Your Subconscious Mind* by Joseph Murphy
- *Return to Love* by Marianne Williamson
- *The Age of Miracles* by Marianne Williamson
- *The Path Towards Self-Awakening* by Neale Donald Walsch
- *Speak and Inspire* by Lisa Nichols
- Angels of Abundance by Doreen Virtue and Grant Virtue
- *The Power of Now* by Eckhart Tolle
- *A New Earth* by Eckhart Tolle
- *The Seven Spiritual Laws of Success* by Deepak Chopra
- *Breaking the Habit of Being Yourself* by Dr. Joe Dispenza
- *Becoming Supernatural* by Dr. Joe Dispenza
- *A Course in Miracles, Made Easy* by Alan Cohen
- *The Miracles of Your Mind* by Joseph Murphy
- *E-Squared* by Pam Grout
- *The 72 Sigils of Power* by Zanna Blaie

- *Angel Detox* by Doreen Virtue & Robert Reeves, N.D.
- *Your Hands Can Heal You* by Master Stephen Co & Eric B. Robins, M.D., with John Merryman
- *Just Ask the Universe* by Michael Samuels
- *It's All Mind* by Edwin Navarro
- *Wisdom from Your Spirit Guides* by James Van Praagh
- *T.N.T. It Rocks the Earth* by Claude M. Bristol
- *Why You're Stuck* by Derek Doepke
- *How to Analyze People* by David Clark
- *You Can Heal Your Life* by Louise Hay
- *Superbrain Yoga* by Master Choa Kok Sui
- *Psychic Development for Beginners* by Grace Loveman
- *Third Eye Activation Mastery* by L. Jordan
- *The Chakras and Their Functions* by Master Choa Kok Sui
- *Clairvoyance* by C. W. Leadbeater
- *The Law of Psychic Phenomena* by Obadiah Switzer
- *Crystal Experience* by Jill Weiss & Jeff Michaels
- *The Magic of Believing* by Claude M. Bristol
- *Wings of Forgiveness* by Kyle Gray
- *Law of Attraction: 30 Practical Exercises* by Louise Stapeley

- *Return to Love* by Yogi Kanna
- *How to Change Your Personality* by Dr. Joe Dispenza
- *Conversations with God, Book 1* by Neale Donald Walsch
- *Conversations with God, Book 2* by Neale Donald Walsch
- *The Disappearance of the Universe* by Gary R. Renard
- *Healer* by Dr. Hazel Parcells

www.ingramcontent.com/pod-product-compliance
Lightning Source LLC
LaVergne TN
LVHW010402070526
838199LV00065B/5876